/2

Stone Circles

Dawn Finch

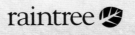

raintree

a Capstone company — publishers for children

Raintree is an imprint of Capstone Global Library Limited, a company incorporated in England and Wales having its registered office at 264 Banbury Road, Oxford, OX2 7DY – Registered company number: 6695582

www.raintree.co.uk
myorders@raintree.co.uk

Edited by Helen Cox Cannons
Designed by Philippa Jenkins
Original illustrations © Capstone Global Library Limited 2017
Picture research by Wanda Winch
Production by Victoria Fitzgerald
Originated by Capstone Global Library Limited
Printed and bound in China

ISBN 978 1 474 73045 7
21 20 19 18 17
10 9 8 7 6 5 4 3 2 1

British Library Cataloguing in Publication Data
A full catalogue record for this book is available from the British Library.

Acknowledgements
All images courtesy of Dawn Finch except: Alamy: Rick Buettner, 16; Capstone, maps; Dreamstime: Wild Exploreruk, 17; Science Source: Sheila Terry, 15; Shutterstock: Anneka, cover, Bablesh Singh, stone background design, Victor Maschek, 28 (bottom); Thinkstock: Wynnter, 14.

The publisher would like to thank Dr Linsey Hunter of the University of the Highlands and Islands for her invaluable help in the preparation of this book. We would also like to thank Eden Joy Finch for her illustration work on page 10.

Contents

Some words in this book appear in bold, like this. You can find out what they mean by looking in the glossary.

What are stone circles?

A stone circle is a **monument** made up of large stones. The stones are arranged so that they are standing in a circle. We call these stones **megaliths**. The oldest stone circles were put up in a period of history known as the **Neolithic** period.

Neolithic means "New Stone Age", which means that it was the end of the Stone Age. The Neolithic period in Britain lasted from around 4000 BC to around 2200 BC. This was followed by the **Bronze Age**. Bronze Age people continued to use the circles and add to them.

Building a picture

Neolithic people did not have a written language that we understand. We do not know much about their lives. This means we cannot know exactly how they used stone circles. **Archaeologists** have been trying to understand more about stone circles for centuries.

ORKNEY ISLANDS
Ring of Brodgar
Stones of Stenness

Calanais

Loanhead of Daviot
Easter Aquhorthies

SCOTLAND

NORTHERN
IRELAND

SOUTHERN
IRELAND
(EIRE)

ENGLAND

WALES

Avebury
Stonehenge

Sittaford Tor

N
W — E
S

This map shows where the stone circles mentioned in this book are in the UK.

It is thought that there are over 1,300 stone circles in the United Kingdom. Most of these stone circles, or megaliths, are in Scotland. The oldest stone circles are over 5,000 years old and were built by Neolithic farmers. Today, the stone circles are usually in empty landscapes where they can be seen from a long way off. When they were built, however, the stone circles were probably in the middle of busy **settlements,** where many people lived and farmed.

Prehistoric stone circles have fascinated people for many hundreds of years. Lots of paintings have been made, and stories and poems have been told or written about stone circles.

Why were stone circles built?

There are lots of different ideas about why stone circles were built. Because we do not have any written information from the **Neolithic** period, **archaeologists** have to get information in other ways. They use any **evidence** they can find at the sites to come up with **theories** about the stone circles and why they were built. These theories change as archaeologists find out more about the sites as they **excavate.**

Archaeologists have had many theories over the centuries about why Stonehenge and other stone circles were built.

The Calanais stone circle, on the Scottish island of Lewis, was built in around 3000 BC.

It would have taken a very long time to build the stone circles. Archaeologists believe that stone circles were first built to mark the **boundaries,** or edges, of land. They may have been placed there to show how important the people in that area were. Bones and burials are often found at stone circles. This suggests that they may have been used as special places to bury **ancestors**. Archaeologists also believe that the Neolithic people must have planned the building work carefully.

Stone circles are often arranged to line up with the rising of the sun or the moon at certain times of year. This could mean that the people used them as some kind of calendar or clock. There is evidence to show that stone circles were also used for **rituals** and religious ceremonies. There is no doubt that the stones were very special places to the people who built them and lived near them.

Who built the stone circles?

During the Stone Age, people were nomadic. This means that they did not settle down in one fixed home but moved from place to place. During the **Neolithic** period, from around 4500 BC, people began to settle in one place and build houses in **settlements**.

These Neolithic people became farmers. They started to grow crops and keep animals for food. They cut down trees and cleared large rocks or stones from the land to prepare it for farming. Archaeologists believe that the farmers used these stones to mark out their land, and many were stood upright to create stone circles. The stone circles were probably quite small at first, but became bigger as the settlements grew larger.

The Neolithic village of Skara Brae lies on the Scottish Orkney Islands. It gives us an idea of what life was like for Neolithic people. This is a model of a home there.

Barrows

When Neolithic people died, they were buried in **mounds** made from earth and rocks. These burial mounds are called **barrows.** Some of the barrows had very large stones in front of the entrances. The Neolithic people began marking their land with standing stones and then began to build stone circles.

West Kennet Long Barrow

This Neolithic barrow at West Kennet, Avebury, Wiltshire, was built in around 3650 BC. It has very large stones at the entrance. The barrow is very long and was used for the burial of up to 50 Neolithic people. When the barrow was full, the entrance tunnel of the barrow was filled up with small stones and earth. The barrow was then closed up tightly and three huge stones were put over the entrance to stop anyone else getting in.

How were stone circles built?

Neolithic people moved the stones for the biggest stone circles across great distances. The stones were cut and shaped in **quarries** many kilometres away. People used the natural cracks in the rocks to split the stones. Then they used simple tools made of stone and wood to smooth and shape the rock.

Standing the stones

To **erect** a stone, the Neolithic people first had to dig a hole behind it. They then tied ropes around the stone and pulled it into place. When the stone was standing upright, they filled in the hole with rocks to hold it in place.

This illustration shows how Neolithic people may have moved and placed the stones.

This model of a wooden roller shows how the largest stone blocks may have been moved.

To move the stones, the Neolithic people would have either floated them down rivers on wooden rafts or dragged them across land on wooden rollers. Some of these stones weigh many thousands of kilograms. It is thought that hundreds of strong people worked together to move the stones and stand them upright. It could have taken many years to move all of the stones into place and would have taken a huge amount of effort.

Types of stone circle

There are two main types of stone circle: **concentric** circles and **recumbent** circles.

Concentric stone circles

Concentric stone circles have their stones standing in a circle or an oval shape. Some of these circles have a smaller circle inside the outer ring. Many of them have a ditch around the outside of the circle.

Many concentric circles also have a pathway leading up to the circle. This pathway is known as an avenue. Most of the concentric circles also have a **mound** in the middle of the circle. All of the **excavations** on these mounds have found burial sites underneath them.

The Stones of Stenness in Orkney are arranged as a concentric circle.

Recumbent stone circles

Recumbent stone circles are mainly found in Scotland and Ireland. These circles have at least one large stone that has been laid on its side. This stone often has a pair of tall stones standing on either side of it. Sometimes these circles have another small circle inside and there may be a burial site in the middle.

Loanhead of Daviot

The recumbent stone at the circle in Daviot, Aberdeenshire, is thought to weigh 20,000 kilograms. It is one of the largest recumbent stones ever found. The stone is now in two parts, as it has been split by cold weather. The giant recumbent stone and the two standing stones either side of it frame the rising of the moon at certain times of the year. This shows us that Neolithic people believed that the moon was important.

Discovery and excavation

Because stone circles are above the ground, they have been explored throughout history. The first people to **excavate** Stonehenge in Wiltshire, England (see pages 20–21), believed that it was built by the Romans. We now know that this is wrong: it was built during the **Neolithic** period.

The first excavation of Stonehenge began in the 1620s. This was upon the orders of King James I of England (also James VI of Scotland), who visited the circle and wanted to know more about it.

Inigo Jones (1573–1652) was royal architect to King James I. In his book about Stonehenge, he claimed that it was actually a temple built by the Romans.

At the end of the 1600s, a historian named John Aubrey (1626–1697) made other excavations. He found a ring of five chalk-filled holes around the main ring of Stonehenge.

Aubrey thought that the circles were built by ancient peoples called the Druids, but the circles were even older than that. It was not until the 1920s that **archaeologists** investigated the chalk-filled holes properly. They found that there were 56 of these holes. They named them Aubrey Holes, after John Aubrey. Archaeologists are still unsure about what the Aubrey Holes were for.

John Aubrey's discovery of chalk-filled holes was not looked into by archaeologists until centuries later.

Modern excavations

Digital technology has been very useful for archaeologists. It has filled in a lot of gaps in our knowledge of stone circles, including how old stone circles are.

Many archaeologists also now make use of technology that can help them look beneath the ground before they begin to dig. An electrical current is passed through the soil and then collected by special equipment. The information gathered can help scientists to make a sort of map of what might be under the ground.

Archaeologists also find out information by doing traditional digs. This dig by archaeologists took place at Avebury.

Sittaford Tor was the first stone circle to be discovered in the UK in over 100 years.

The UK has thousands of ancient sites, and archaeology groups from all over the world work hard to explore them. Even with modern technology, most of the work is still done by experts carefully digging and exploring by hand.

Sometimes, amazing things are found quite by accident! In May 2015, a new **Bronze Age** stone circle was discovered at Sittaford Tor in Dartmoor, England. It was found after an area of wild moorland was cleared by fire. The stones had all fallen over and been covered in earth and heather.

Ring of Brodgar

The Ring of Brodgar is a stone circle that was built during the **Neolithic** period between 2500 BC and 2000 BC. It is on the Scottish island of Orkney.

The Ring of Brodgar is part of the **World Heritage site** called the Heart of Neolithic Orkney. Within the Heart of Neolithic Orkney are many other Neolithic sites, including the Stones of Stenness and the Neolithic village of Skara Brae.

The stones in the Ring of Brodgar are mostly tall standing stones, but some are smaller and shaped differently.

The Ring of Brodgar is a large circular ring of stones with a bank and ditch that runs all the way around it. This means that it is a stone circle in a **henge**. It is one of the largest stone circles and once had more than 60 stones. The circle is 104 metres (340 feet) wide. That means the area within the circles is nearly as big as a football pitch! Today, 36 stones are still standing. The tallest stone stands at 4.7 metres (15 feet) tall — that's around 2.5 times the height of the average adult man.

The Ring is on the edge of two **lochs** that are joined by a thin strip of land. When it was built, only one of the lochs existed and the area next to the stones would have been **marshy** land. Archaeologists have discovered at least 13 burial **mounds** close to the site, but the centre of the ring has not yet been fully **excavated**. We do not know if there is a burial site in the middle of the ring.

The Stones of Stenness

The Stones of Stenness is a stone circle that stands not far from the Ring of Brodgar. It is thought to be the oldest stone circle in the British Isles. It was probably built between 3000 BC and 2900 BC. Only 4 of the circle's 12 stones are still standing. The tallest of these (shown here) reaches a massive height of 6 metres (20 feet).

Stonehenge

Stonehenge is one of the most famous **prehistoric monuments** in the world. It stands on Salisbury Plain in Wiltshire, England. It is in the middle of a landscape full of burial **mounds** and other **Neolithic** sites.

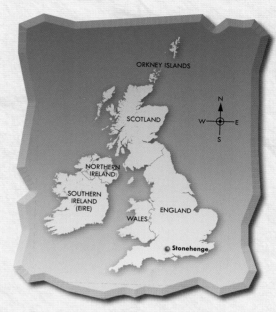

People began to build Stonehenge in around 2800 BC, but it took many hundreds of years to finish. It began with a ditch, or **henge**, and then a single ring of small stones. After that, Neolithic people put up a ring of very large stones and hundreds of years later another two rings of stones. The last stage of building was the massive ring of stones that people recognize it for today. The giant stones can be seen from kilometres away.

trilithon
(two standing sarsen stones topped with a lintel)

bluestones

sarsen stones

Hundreds of people would have worked together to build Stonehenge. The **bluestones** in the inner ring were brought from quarries over 300 kilometres (186 miles) away. There are 29 bluestones that can be seen today, but there may have been up to 80 at one time. The bluestones weigh up to 4,000 kilograms each. They may have been pulled on sledges with wooden rollers, or floated up rivers on rafts.

The 15 huge standing stones, called sarsens, weigh up to 25,000 kilograms and were brought to the site from up to 50 kilometres (31 miles) away. Some of the sarsen stones have a **lintel** joining them together – this is called a trilithon. In the past Stonehenge may have had as many as 160 stones.

What is a henge?

We call Stonehenge a henge, but it is really a stone circle that is built inside a henge. A henge is the name for a human-made circular or oval area surrounded by a ditch and bank.

low ditch

Avebury

Avebury stone circle in Wiltshire is the largest stone circle in England. It was built around 2850–2200 BC. The circle is more than 400 metres (1,312 feet) wide. It is so big that houses have been built inside it! The ditch and banks around the edge of the circle are huge.

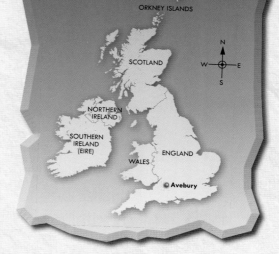

Today, the bank is over 5 metres (16 feet) high, but when it was built it was nearly 17 metres (56 feet) and the ditch was more than 9 metres (30 feet) deep. Over time, the ditch was filled in with rubbish or may have collapsed. The earth is very chalky and the bank would have been a dazzling white. It could be seen from a great distance.

Today, sheep wander freely in the Avebury circle. They use the stones for shade and shelter.

There are actually three large stone circles at Avebury: the Outer Ring, the Southern Circle and the Northern Circle. The Outer Ring had over 100 stones, the Southern Circle had 30 stones and the Northern Circle probably had 27 stones. Avebury also had a long avenue of stones and there may have once been more than 600 stones in all.

The bank around the Avebury stone circle is taller than the houses in some places!

Around 200 years ago, local people broke up many of the stones at Avebury. They used the stones to build their houses. One of the avenues has gone completely but **archaeologists** have managed to work out where it would have been. Thankfully, many of the stones were far too big to move.

Some of the stones at Avebury are very large indeed. The stones called the Cove Stones are over 5 metres (16 feet) tall and could weigh as much as 50,000 kilograms. That is heavier than three London buses full of people!

23

Calanais

The Calanais stone circle was built on the Scottish island of Lewis around 3000 BC. Calanais is also known as Callanish.

Calanais is an unusual stone circle because the stones in the centre are arranged in a cross shape. In the centre, there is a taller stone known as a **monolith**. Lines of smaller stones lead out from the circle and form avenues in different directions. The avenue to the north stretches for 83 metres (272 feet). In the middle of the circle, there is a small burial place called a **cairn**.

You might recognize this stone circle. It was the inspiration for the stone circle in the Disney film *Brave* (2012)!

In ancient times, the land around Calanais became flooded with seawater. This made the marshland salty and not good for farming. This led to people moving away from the circle.

The landscape of Lewis has very few trees. Calanais was built on a **ridge** of land and can be seen from many kilometres away. It is in a landscape where there are many other standing stones and ancient **monuments**. It is thought that Calanais was possibly built as a way of following the seasons or the stars.

About 1,000 years after it was built, people stopped using Calanais. The centre area was cleared and the land was farmed. In time, a thick layer of **peat** formed around the stones and they became half-buried. When the peat was cut back in 1857, people were surprised to discover how tall the stones really were.

Easter Aquhorthies

Easter Aquhorthies is a **recumbent** stone circle in Aberdeenshire, north-east Scotland. Recumbent stone circles are found only in the north-east of Scotland, and the far south-west of Ireland.

It is believed that people built the stone circle at Easter Aquhorthies around 3000 BC. The large recumbent stone was then put in place almost 1,000 years later. The recumbent stone itself is made of red granite, which has a pinkish colour. It is 3.8 metres (12 feet) long and weighs around 9,000 kilograms. This is heavier than an African elephant! Either side of the recumbent stone, there are two standing stones known as flanking stones.

This is the huge recumbent stone at Easter Aquhorthies.

This is the only stone made from red jasper. The stone normally looks quite pink, but when it rains you can easily see the red colour.

The stones in the Easter Aquhorthies circle are mostly made of a cream-coloured stone called porphyry. One of the stones is made of red jasper and it looks very different to the other, paler stones. The flanking stones either side of the recumbent stone are made of grey granite and are more than 2 metres (6 feet) tall.

Many of the stones in the circle were brought from a **quarry** near a hill fort several kilometres away. This hill, named Bennachie, can be seen in the distance from the stone circle. It is not known how the huge stones were brought down from the hill and all the way to where they stand today.

Visiting stone circles

Most of the UK's stone circles are free to visit and have signs explaining the history of the site. There is a fee to visit Stonehenge. Nearly 1 million people visit it every year, and there is plenty to see and do. There are reconstructions (models) of **Neolithic** houses there and a display showing the history of the site.

If you visit a stone circle, look out for some of the things mentioned in this book. Have a look to see if it is a **recumbent** stone circle or a **concentric** stone circle, and see if you can find the **henge**. Some stones may have carvings on them. These might only be a shallow dip called a cup carving, or simple lines or circles.

Cup carvings at Loanhead of Daviot

Stone circles are a fascinating link to the past of our ancient **ancestors**. Visiting them brings the past to life.

Stonehenge is in the top ten most-visited places in the UK.

Timeline

BC

About 4200	First farming people arrive in Britain from Europe
About 4000	**Neolithic,** or New Stone Age, begins
About 3650	West Kennet Long **Barrow** burial site is built
About 3200	First building work begins at the Neolithic village of Skara Brae
3000–2900	Stones of Stenness are put in place
About 3000	Calanais stone circle, also known as Callanish, is built
About 3000	Stone circle at Loanhead of Daviot is built
3000	The Easter Aquhorthies stones are put in place
2850–2200	Avebury stone circle is put in place
2800	First stones of Stonehenge are put in place
2500–2000	The Ring of Brodgar stone circle is built
2200	The **Bronze Age** begins in Britain

AD

1620s	King James I of England and VI of Scotland visits Stonehenge and orders an **excavation** of the site
late 1600s	John Aubrey makes further excavations of the Stonehenge site
1850	Neolithic village of Skara Brae is discovered
2014	Stonehenge Hidden Landscape project reveals new stone **monument** 3 kilometres (1.8 miles) away from the main stone circle
2015	New Bronze Age stone circle is discovered at Sittaford Tor in Dartmoor, England

Glossary

ancestor member of your family who has been dead for a long time

archaeologist scientist who studies human history by digging up people's buildings, belongings and even their bones

barrow burial mound made from earth and rocks

bluestones smaller standing stones used in the building of Stonehenge

Bronze Age period in history after the Stone Age that lasted from around 2200 BC to 800 BC

cairn small stones piled up as a monument, burial or landmark

concentric circles or other shapes that share the same centre. In concentric stone circles, the larger circles often completely surround the smaller ones.

erect stand something upright

evidence object that proves something existed or happened

excavate uncover something by digging or removing soil

henge circular area surrounded by a bank and ditch

lintel supporting beam or stone, usually at the top of a door or window

loch Scottish lake or part of the sea that is largely surrounded by land

marshy low and very wet area of land, often with long grasses and reeds

megalith large stone used as a monument

monolith very large block of stone

monument something built in memory of a person or an event

mound small hill, usually made from piles of gravel, sand or rocks, and covered with earth and grass

Neolithic later part of the Stone Age, between around 4000 BC and 2200 BC

peat soil from a wet area that is made up of rotted plants

prehistoric something that is kept safe and protected from harm

quarries places where people cut large rocks for use elsewhere

recumbent lying down

ridge long, narrow, raised section at the top of a hill or slope

rituals set of actions that are performed in the same way, often for religious purposes

settlement place where a group of people lived

theory unproven statement that explains how or why something happened

World Heritage Site place recognized by the United Nations Educational Scientific and Cultural Organisation (UNESCO) as having special historical, physical or cultural importance

Find out more

Books

Changes in Britain from the Stone Age to the Iron Age (Early British History), Claire Throp (Raintree, 2015)
Life in the Stone Age, Bronze Age and Iron Age (A Child's History of Britain), Anita Ganeri (Raintree, 2014)
Stone Circles (Prehistoric Adventures), John Malam (Wayland, 2016)

Websites

www.bbc.co.uk/guides/zg8q2hv
This interactive website from the BBC contains lots of facinating information about Stonehenge.

www.educationscotland.gov.uk/scotlandshistory/earlypeople/index.asp
This website about Scottish history includes photographs, illustrations and information about prehistoric sites, including Calanais and the Ring of Brodgar.

www.historic-scotland.gov.uk
Historic Scotland is responsible for taking care of some stone circles and many other ancient sites across Scotland.

www.orkneyjar.com
This website includes contributions from the archaeologists who have been excavating the ancient sites in Orkney.

Index